INSIDE THE
NFL

NEW ENGLAND
PATRIOTS

BY ROBERT COOPER

SportsZone

An Imprint of Abdo Publishing
abdobooks.com

abdobooks.com

Published by Abdo Publishing, a division of ABDO, PO Box 398166, Minneapolis, Minnesota 55439. Copyright © 2020 by Abdo Consulting Group, Inc. International copyrights reserved in all countries. No part of this book may be reproduced in any form without written permission from the publisher. SportsZone™ is a trademark and logo of Abdo Publishing.

Printed in the United States of America, North Mankato, Minnesota
042019
092019

THIS BOOK CONTAINS
RECYCLED MATERIALS

Cover Photo: Jim Mahoney/AP Images
Interior Photos: Tony Gutierrez/AP Images, 5; Jae C. Hong/AP Images, 7; G. Newman Lowrance/AP Images, 9, 43; Focus on Sport/Getty Images Sport/Getty Images, 11; Herb Scharfman/Sports Illustrated/Set Number: X12076/Getty Images, 14; Donald Preston/The Boston Globe/Getty Images, 16; Doug Jennings/AP Images, 19; NFL Photos/AP Images, 20; Ray Stubblebine/AP Images, 23; Doug Mills/AP Images, 25; Elaine Thompson/AP Images, 27; Steven Senne/AP Images, 29; Amy Sancetta/AP Images, 30–31; Tom DiPace/AP Images, 32; Dave Martin/AP Images, 35; Ben Liebenberg/AP Images, 36; Chuck Burton/AP Images, 40

Editor: Patrick Donnelly
Series Designer: Craig Hinton

Library of Congress Control Number: 2018965648

Publisher's Cataloging-in-Publication Data

Names: Cooper, Robert, author.
Title: New England Patriots / by Robert Cooper
Description: Minneapolis, Minnesota: Abdo Publishing, 2020 | Series: Inside the NFL | Includes online resources and index.
Identifiers: ISBN 9781532118579 (lib. bdg.) | ISBN 9781532172755 (ebook) | ISBN 9781644941119 (pbk.)
Subjects: LCSH: New England Patriots (Football team)--Juvenile literature. | National Football League--Juvenile literature. | Football teams--Juvenile literature. | American football--Juvenile literature.
Classification: DDC 796.33264--dc23

TABLE OF
CONTENTS

CHAPTER 1

A COMEBACK
FOR THE AGES

Tom Brady and the New England Patriots took the field midway through the third quarter of the Super Bowl. After a strong 2016 season, New England had advanced to its second Super Bowl in three seasons. But so far that day, the Atlanta Falcons had been having their way with the Patriots.

Brady had thrown an interception that the Falcons returned for a touchdown. The Patriots defense had just given up its third touchdown drive of the day. New England trailed the Falcons 28–3.

But Brady refused to quit. He completed pass after pass, capping the drive with a short touchdown pass to James White. The Patriots missed the extra-point kick, and Atlanta led 28–9.

Tom Brady used his legs to help the Patriots get back into the game against Atlanta.

As the fourth quarter began, Atlanta held its 19-point lead. Once again, Brady and the Patriots got the ball back. After reaching the Atlanta 7-yard line, Brady was sacked twice, and the Patriots had to settle for a field goal to make it 28–12.

Inside Houston's NRG Stadium, momentum was shifting. Minutes later, Falcons quarterback Matt Ryan was hit as he tried to throw. He fumbled and New England recovered. The Patriots had the ball deep in Atlanta territory with eight minutes to go. But they still trailed by 16 points.

Five plays later, Brady connected with Danny Amendola. The Patriots wide receiver dove for the goal line and scored a touchdown. When New England picked up the two-point conversion on a run by White, they trailed 28–20 with just under six minutes to play.

The Falcons fought back. They drove inside the New England 25-yard line, well within kicker Matt Bryant's range. A field goal would push the lead to 11, forcing

TOM TERRIFIC

Tom Brady was a sixth-round pick in the 2000 National Football League (NFL) Draft. The Patriots selected Brady out of the University of Michigan as a backup to starting quarterback Drew Bledsoe. But in 2001, Brady was thrown into the spotlight when Bledsoe was injured. That season, Brady became the second quarterback in NFL history to win a Super Bowl in his first season as a starting quarterback.

✕ Julian Edelman, *center*, makes an acrobatic catch between two Atlanta defenders during the Super Bowl.

New England to score twice to tie or take the lead. Then disaster struck the Falcons. The Patriots sacked Ryan, and on the next play a holding penalty pushed the Falcons back 10 more yards. Atlanta was forced to punt. New England took over at its own 9-yard line with 3:30 remaining.

The Patriots moved quickly. Brady completed passes to five different receivers on the drive. The most memorable catch was made by wide receiver Julian Edelman. The ball tipped off the hands of a Falcons defensive back. It looked like it was going to fall to the ground for an incomplete pass. Instead, Edelman dove for the ball and hauled it in for a reception.

A TALENTED TRIO

During Tom Brady's first 18 seasons in New England, the Patriots quarterback was almost always in the lineup. But while Brady was consistent, he played with a rotating cast of running backs. The 2016 season was no different. The Patriots succeeded that year with three running backs: James White, LeGarrette Blount, and Dion Lewis. Each one had his moments during the season. In the Super Bowl, White caught 14 passes for 110 yards and a touchdown. He also scored two rushing touchdowns that day.

New England soon reached the Atlanta 1-yard line. White scooted into the end zone for a touchdown to cut Atlanta's lead to 28–26. The Patriots went for two on the next play. Brady's quick toss to Amendola tied the game. The clock ran out with the score 28–28.

This was history in the making. No team had ever come back from 25 points down in the Super Bowl. And no Super Bowl had ever gone into overtime.

New England won the coin toss and elected to take the ball first. Three minutes into overtime,

✖ James White scores the winning touchdown in Super Bowl LI.

the Patriots had the ball inside the Atlanta 5-yard line. After
an incomplete pass attempt to tight end Martellus Bennett,
Brady tossed the ball back to White. Running to his right, White
spotted an opening. He burrowed through the Falcons defense
and put the ball over the goal line for the game-winning
touchdown. The Patriots had their fifth Super Bowl title in
franchise history in a dramatic 34–28 win.

After taking over as the team's starting quarterback in 2001,
Brady led New England to success the team had never seen
before. He broke countless records while also putting an end to
the Patriots' long history of heartbreak.

CHAPTER 2

FROM BOSTON TO
FOXBOROUGH

On November 16, 1959, Boston was awarded a professional football team. A group of local businessmen was given the eighth and final team in the new American Football League (AFL). The AFL was a rival league to the more established NFL.

The team was not originally known as the New England Patriots. Instead, they were called the Boston Patriots after locals were allowed to submit ideas for the name. Later, a mascot was chosen based on a drawing by an artist from the *Boston Globe* newspaper. The mascot was called "Pat Patriot." The logo showed a minuteman snapping a football. The minutemen were members of the American colonial militia during the American Revolutionary War (1775–1783).

Boston kicker and wide receiver Gino Cappelletti (20) led the AFL in scoring five times.

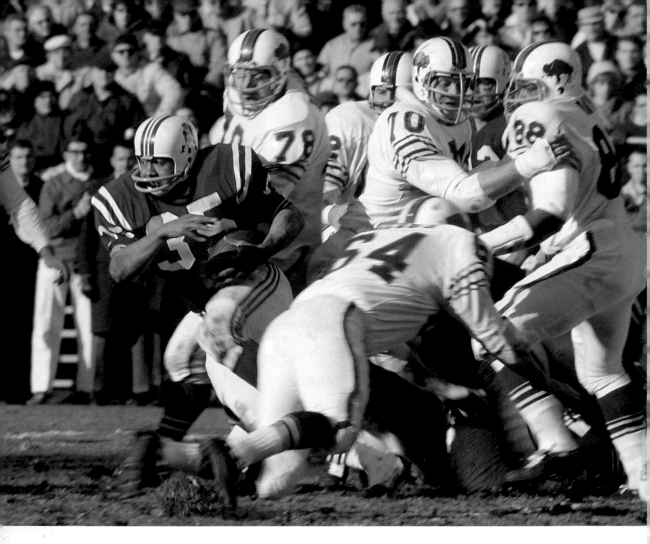

✕ Patriots running back Jim Nance (35) breaks out of a pack of Buffalo Bills defenders.

The rest of the 1960s brought mixed results for the Patriots. Some of the team's standouts included wide receiver and kicker Gino Cappelletti, running back Jim Nance, linebacker Nick Buoniconti, and defensive lineman Bob Dee. The Patriots went 10–3–1 but finished in second place to the Bills in the Eastern Division in 1964. Boston went 8–4–2 in 1966 and again finished runner-up to Buffalo in the East. In 1969 the Patriots moved to Alumni Stadium on the Boston College campus.

Many big changes occurred for the Patriots in the early 1970s. First the AFL and NFL merged to form a larger NFL in 1970. The Patriots would compete in the American Football Conference (AFC) East—one of three divisions in the AFC. Joining the Patriots in the AFC East were the Bills, the Baltimore Colts, the Miami Dolphins, and the New York Jets. Boston finished its first season in the NFL just 2–12. The Patriots had a new home stadium again, playing at Harvard Stadium in Boston.

Then, in 1970, the Patriots announced they were moving from Boston to the suburbs. Beginning in 1971, the team would play its home games at the new Schaefer Stadium in Foxborough.

With the move out of Boston and into Foxborough came a new name for the team. On March 22, 1971, the board of directors voted to rename the team the New England Patriots.

The Patriots struggled for several seasons. But they were adding talented players through the draft. Among them were guard John Hannah, tight end Russ Francis, quarterback Steve Grogan, and cornerback Mike Haynes.

Schaefer Stadium is shown in 1971. It opened that year in Foxborough, Massachusetts, and became the Patriots' home.

Grogan became their starting quarterback partway through his rookie season in 1975. By 1976 enough pieces were in place for New England to go 11–3 and qualify for its first NFL playoff appearance. The Patriots, under head coach Chuck Fairbanks, earned a wild-card playoff berth. Despite trailing 21–10 in the fourth quarter, the host Oakland Raiders rallied to edge the Patriots 24–21 in the first round.

The Patriots returned to the playoffs in 1978. That season they went 11–5 and captured the first outright division title in team history. The Patriots hosted their first playoff game ever. But they lost 31–14 to the Houston Oilers. After the 1978 season, Fairbanks left to become coach at the University of Colorado. He was replaced by Patriots offensive coordinator Ron Erhardt.

The Patriots were starting to show signs of progress. The team would knock on the door of big-time success in the 1980s.

STINGLEY'S INJURY

On August 12, 1978, during an exhibition game against the host Oakland Raiders, Patriots wide receiver Darryl Stingley suffered an injury that left him paralyzed below his neck. Stingley, trying to catch a pass over the middle, was defenseless when he was hit by Raiders safety Jack Tatum. Tragically, the impact of the hit drove several of Stingley's vertebrae together, causing paralysis. In time, Stingley regained limited movement in his right arm. He recovered well enough to serve as the Patriots' executive director of player personnel. In 1983 he published his memoir *Happy to Be Alive*. Stingley's paralysis was a contributing factor when he died in 2007 at age 55.

CHAPTER 3

GETTING TO THE
SUPER BOWL

The Patriots had their first taste of the NFL playoffs after the 1976 and 1978 seasons. They won a combined 19 games in 1979 and 1980 but just missed the playoffs each year.

New England slumped to 2–14 in 1981 but rebounded in 1982. The season was shortened to nine games due to a players' strike. The Patriots finished 5–4 and qualified for a postseason berth. However, they lost 28–13 to the host Miami Dolphins in the first round. New England was still winless in the playoffs in the NFL.

The Patriots hovered near .500 and missed the playoffs the next two years. Four games into the 1984 season New England decided to go with second-year quarterback Tony Eason over the aging Steve Grogan.

Head coach Raymond Berry is carried off the field after the Patriots beat the Dolphins in the AFC title game.

at the Orange Bowl in Miami. Though the Patriots played their divisional foes there every season, New England had not won at the Orange Bowl since 1966—in Miami's first season in the AFL.

New England ended that streak emphatically. Craig James had 105 of the Patriots' 255 rushing yards. Eason threw for three touchdowns. Miami's star quarterback Dan Marino completed just 20 of 48 throws and was intercepted twice. The Patriots cruised to a 31–14 victory, becoming the first team to win three road playoff games on the way to the Super Bowl.

Next up were the mighty Chicago Bears in Super Bowl XX in New Orleans. The Bears had gone 15–1 in the regular season and shut out both of their playoff opponents. New England proved to be no match for Chicago. The day before the game, Grogan was medically cleared to play. Berry put Grogan in during the second quarter after Eason started 0-for-6. But it did not matter. The Bears were simply too good.

Chicago held New England to seven rushing yards and intercepted two of Grogan's passes. The Bears also recorded seven sacks, including one for a safety, and recovered four fumbles. Chicago rolled to a 46–10 win.

The next season, New England again finished 11–5 and made the playoffs. This time, however, the Patriots won the

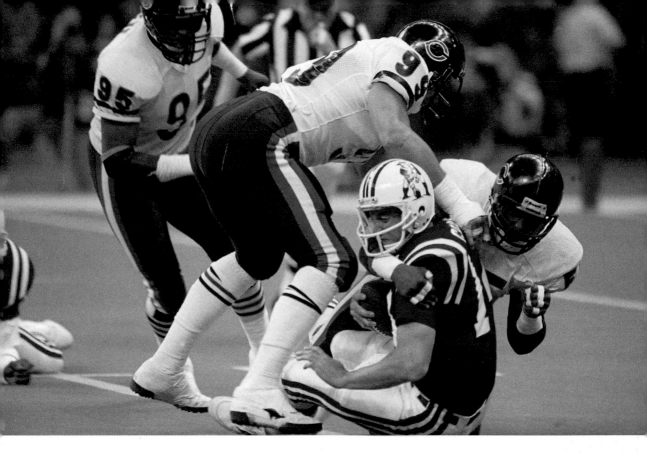

✗ Dan Hampton (99) and Otis Wilson bring down New England quarterback Steve Grogan in Chicago's 46–10 Super Bowl XX win.

AFC East Division. Eason returned as the starting quarterback. New England traveled to Denver to face the Broncos in the postseason's divisional round. Despite two touchdown passes from Eason to Stanley Morgan, the Broncos won 22–17. It marked the last time that New England would make the playoffs under Berry. He was fired after the 1989 season.

The 1990s were around the corner. New England had made progress in the 1980s and would make some more in the next decade, though it would not start out well at all.

CHAPTER 4

A PERIOD OF
CHANGE

The Patriots underwent many changes in the years after their Super Bowl debut in January 1986. The changes left the team with new owners, a new coach, and a new look.

Billy Sullivan originally brought the Patriots to Massachusetts in 1959. He sold the team to businessman Victor Kiam in July 1988. The Patriots suffered through a team-worst 1–15 season in 1990. Kiam sold the team before the 1992 campaign to advertising executive James Orthwein, a native of St. Louis, Missouri.

New England continued to struggle. The team finished 2–14 in 1992. Orthwein then hired Bill Parcells as head coach in 1993. Parcells had coached the New York Giants to two Super Bowl wins. The Patriots also announced that instead of

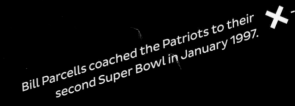

Bill Parcells coached the Patriots to their second Super Bowl in January 1997.

CHAPTER 5

TEAM OF THE CENTURY

As the twenty-first century began, the NFL's ultimate prize—a league title—had remained out of the Patriots' reach. That all changed in the new decade. This was in large part because of two men: Bill Belichick and Tom Brady.

New England hired Belichick as its new head coach on January 27, 2000. He had served once before as an NFL head coach—with the Cleveland Browns from 1991 to 1995. The Browns had just one playoff victory during that time. Belichick fared better as a defensive assistant. This included stints with the Giants, Jets, and Patriots.

New England went 5–11 in Belichick's first season. But the 2001 season was a surprise success. Brady was forced into a leadership role after starter Drew Bledsoe was injured in the

Wide receiver David Givens celebrates during New England's third Super Bowl victory in four years.

seconds left. Belichick sent Vinatieri out for a 48-yard field-goal attempt to win the game. He drilled the kick as time expired for a 20–17 victory. New England was the Super Bowl champion for the first time in team history.

New England went 9–7 in 2002 and just missed the playoffs. The Patriots really hit their stride in 2003, going 14–2 and returning to the Super Bowl, where they had a fight on their hands against the Carolina Panthers. Carolina quarterback Jake Delhomme's 12-yard touchdown pass to Ricky Proehl with 1:08 left tied the score at 29–29.

But once again, Brady coolly led the Patriots into field-goal range. And once again, Vinatieri converted the game-winning kick, this one from 41 yards out with four seconds left. New England won 32–29. Brady passed for 354 yards and three touchdowns. He was named Super Bowl MVP a second time.

New England was back in the Super Bowl in 2004, this time

"SPYGATE"

The Patriots' remarkable 2007 season was not without controversy. The NFL disciplined New England after it was revealed that the team, from its sideline, had videotaped the New York Jets defensive coaches' signals during a game on September 9. The league fined head coach Bill Belichick $500,000 and the team $250,000 and took away a first-round draft pick in 2008.

✗ Adam Vinatieri (4) is mobbed after his clutch field goal lifts New England over Carolina in Super Bowl XXXVIII.

against the Philadelphia Eagles. The Patriots won 24–21. New England wide receiver Deion Branch was the game's MVP. He had 11 catches for 133 yards.

✕ Plaxico Burress of the Giants catches the game–winning touchdown pass to end New England's dreams of an undefeated season in February 2008.

The Patriots had won three Super Bowls in four seasons. They became just the second team to do that, joining the Dallas Cowboys of the 1990s. They had the look of a dynasty in the making. But the Patriots could not add to their Super Bowl count as they came up short in 2005 and 2006.

Before the 2007 season, the Patriots landed volatile wide receiver Randy Moss in a trade. Moss was on his best behavior as New England became the first NFL team to finish a regular season 16–0. The Miami Dolphins went 14–0 in 1972, before the NFL went to a 16-game schedule. New England scored an NFL single-season record 589 points. Brady established a league mark with 50 touchdown passes. Moss set an NFL record with 23 touchdown receptions.

The Patriots tried to join the 1972 Dolphins as the only NFL teams to finish an entire season—regular season and postseason—unbeaten and untied. This time their Super Bowl opponents were the New York Giants. New England was a big favorite, but the game was close throughout. Brady's 6-yard scoring pass to Moss gave the Patriots a 14–10 advantage with 2:42 remaining. Giants quarterback Eli Manning then guided his team on an 83-yard drive. It was capped with Manning's 13-yard touchdown pass to wide receiver Plaxico Burress with 35 seconds left. New York held on to win 17–14.

In 2008 Brady suffered a knee injury in the opening game and missed the rest of the season. Behind backup quarterback Matt Cassel, New England finished 11–5 but missed the playoffs. Brady was back in 2009 but saw the Patriots get blown out in the first round of that year's playoffs. New England was

✕ The Patriots' Stephon Gilmore makes a key interception to help New England beat the Rams in the Super Bowl in February 2019.

Eagles and backup quarterback Nick Foles. In a back-and-forth classic, the teams combined for just one punt and broke the NFL record for most yards in any game with 1,151. Foles and the Eagles came out on top 41–33.

The Patriots won the AFC East for the tenth straight year in 2018. And after rolling past the Los Angeles Chargers in the divisional round 41–28, the Patriots went on the road for the AFC Championship Game. They took on the Kansas City Chiefs, the team with the best record in the conference and the eventual league MVP, quarterback Patrick Mahomes. After a slow start, the teams lit up the scoreboard in the second half and ended regulation tied 31–31.

New England won the coin toss and got the ball first in overtime. The Patriots marched to the Kansas City 2-yard line in 12 plays. Then running back Rex Burkhead scored to give the Patriots a 37–31 win.

In the Super Bowl, New England went up against another rising young quarterback in Jared Goff and the Los Angeles Rams. In the lowest-scoring Super Bowl ever, New England got a pair of Stephen Gostkowski field goals and a lights-out performance by its defense in a 13–3 win. Edelman was named the game's MVP as he racked up 10 catches for 141 yards.

With the victory, New England joined the Pittsburgh Steelers as the only teams to win six Super Bowls. All of them came with Belichick as head coach and Brady as quarterback. It was a stretch of success that had never been seen before.

TIMELINE

The Patriots announce on April 4 that they will move to a new stadium in suburban Foxborough for the 1971 season.

The Patriots lose to the San Diego Chargers 51–10 in the AFL Championship Game on January 5.

The Patriots lose 13–10 to the visiting Denver Broncos in their first regular-season game on September 9.

After a public contest, the team is officially named the Patriots and the team colors of red, white, and blue are chosen on February 20.

Boston is awarded the eighth team in the new AFL on November 16.

1959
1960
1960
1964
1970

Former Patriots assistant coach Bill Belichick is named the Patriots' head coach on January 27.

New England loses 35–21 to the Green Bay Packers in Super Bowl XXXI on January 26.

Former New York Giants head coach Bill Parcells is named the head coach of the Patriots on January 21.

New England loses 46–10 to the Chicago Bears in the Super Bowl on January 26.

The Boston Patriots are renamed the New England Patriots on March 22.

1971
1986
1993
1997
2000

The Patriots and second-year quarterback Tom Brady win their first NFL title with a 20–17 victory over the St. Louis Rams on February 3.

✕
2002

New England defeats the Carolina Panthers 32–29 on February 1 in the Super Bowl.

✕
2004

The Patriots win their third Super Bowl, defeating the Philadelphia Eagles 24–21 on February 6.

✕
2005

On December 29, New England becomes the first team in NFL history to finish a regular season 16–0 with a 38–35 win over the New York Giants.

✕
2007

The Giants upset the Patriots 17–14 in Super Bowl XLII on February 3.

✕
2008

On February 5, New England loses another Super Bowl to the Giants, 21–17.

✕
2012

The Patriots win their first Super Bowl in nearly a decade, defeating Seattle 28–24 on February 1.

✕
2015

After trailing the Falcons 28–3, the Patriots complete the biggest comeback in Super Bowl history to win 34–28 on February 5.

✕
2017

On February 4, the Patriots lose to the Philadelphia Eagles 41–33 in the Super Bowl.

✕
2018

New England defeats the Los Angeles Rams 13–3 to win its sixth Super Bowl championship on February 3.

✕
2019

43

QUICK STATS

FRANCHISE HISTORY

Boston Patriots, 1960–69 (AFL)
Boston Patriots, 1970 (NFL)
New England Patriots, 1971– (NFL)

SUPER BOWLS
(wins in bold)

1985 (XX), 1996 (XXXI),
2001 (XXXVI), 2003 (XXXVIII),
2004 (XXXIX), 2007 (XLII),
2011 (XLVI), **2014 (XLIX), 2016 (LI),**
2017 (LII), **2018 (LIII)**

AFL CHAMPIONSHIP
GAMES (1960–69)

1963

AFC CHAMPIONSHIP
GAMES (since 1970
AFL-NFL merger)

1985, 1996, 2001, 2003, 2004, 2006,
2007, 2011, 2012, 2013, 2014, 2015,
2016, 2017, 2018

KEY COACHES

Bill Belichick (2000–): 225–79,
30–10 (playoffs)
Raymond Berry (1984–89): 48–39,
3–2 (playoffs)
Bill Parcells (1993–96): 32–32,
2–2 (playoffs)

KEY PLAYERS (position,
seasons with team)

Drew Bledsoe (QB, 1993–2001)
Tom Brady (QB, 2000–)
Tedy Bruschi (LB, 1996–2008)
Nick Buoniconti (LB, 1962–68)
Gino Cappelletti (K/WR, 1960–70)
Julian Edelman (WR, 2009–)
Steve Grogan (QB, 1975–90)
Rob Gronkowski (TE, 2010–18)
John Hannah (G, 1973–85)
Mike Haynes (CB, 1976–82)
Ty Law (CB, 1995–2004)
Matt Light (LT, 2001–11)
Logan Mankins (G, 2005–13)
Stanley Morgan (WR, 1977–89)
Andre Tippett (LB, 1982–93)
Adam Vinatieri (K, 1996–2005)
Wes Welker (WR, 2007–12)
Vince Wilfork (DT, 2004–14)

HOME FIELDS

Gillette Stadium (2002–)
Foxboro Stadium (1971–2001)
    Also known as Sullivan Stadium
    and Schaefer Stadium
Harvard Stadium (1970)
Alumni Stadium (1969)
Fenway Park (1963–68)
Nickerson Field (1960–62)

*All statistics through 2018 season

New England head coach Bill Belichick was not the first coach in his family. His father, Steve, played fullback for the Detroit Lions in 1941 and scouted and served as an assistant coach for the US Naval Academy team for 33 years.

After Tom Brady received a four-game suspension for his part in the Deflategate controversy, many Patriots fans were angry at NFL commissioner Roger Goodell. When New England won the Super Bowl that season, fans booed Goodell as he handed the Vince Lombardi Trophy to the team. The following season, Patriots fans wore shirts and waved towels that featured Goodell's face with a clown nose on it.

"At the risk of sounding immodest, I believe we are the team of the decade."

—Patriots owner Robert Kraft, on his team's success in the 2000s

On December 12, 1982, a snowstorm hit New England during the Patriots game against the Miami Dolphins. The playing conditions were terrible. The game was still scoreless with 4:45 left when Patriots kicker John Smith prepared to attempt a 33-yard field goal. During a break in the action, New England head coach Ron Meyer ordered a snowplow operator to clear a spot on the field. He did, and Smith converted the kick. Dolphins head coach Don Shula protested furiously. But the kick stood. New England won 3–0. The contest is now referred to as "the Snowplow Game." The next year, the NFL banned the use of snowplows on the field.

GLOSSARY

berth
A place, spot, or position, such as in the NFL playoffs.

draft
A system that allows teams to acquire new players coming into a league.

dynasty
A team that has an extended period of success, usually winning multiple championships in the process.

franchise
A sports organization, including the top-level team and all minor league affiliates.

general manager
A team employee responsible for negotiating contracts with that team's players.

postseason
Another word for playoffs; the time after the end of the regular season when teams play to determine a champion.

rookie
A professional athlete in his or her first year of competition.

sack
A tackle of the quarterback behind the line of scrimmage before he can pass the ball.

MORE INFORMATION

FURTHER READING

Christopher, Matt. *On the Field with … Tom Brady*. New York: Little, Brown and Company, 2018.

Scheff, Matt. *New England Patriots*. Minneapolis, MN: Abdo Publishing, 2017.

Wilner, Barry. *Tom Brady and the New England Patriots*. Minneapolis, MN: Abdo Publishing, 2019.

ONLINE RESOURCES

Booklinks
NONFICTION NETWORK
FREE! ONLINE NONFICTION RESOURCES

To learn more about the New England Patriots, visit **abdobooklinks.com** or scan this QR code. These links are routinely monitored and updated to provide the most current information available.

PLACE TO VISIT

Patriots Hall of Fame
2 Patriot Place
Foxborough, MA 02035
508–698–4800
patriotshalloffame.com

This Hall of Fame gives fans a chance to check out the history of the Patriots through interactive exhibits and memorabilia. The Hall opened in 2008.

INDEX

ABOUT THE AUTHOR

Robert Cooper is a retired law enforcement officer and lifelong NFL fan. He and his wife live in Seattle near their only son and two grandchildren.